THE DRUMS

By Felipe Drago

Edited by Joe Bergamini
Executive producers: Dom Famularo and Joe Bergamini
Layout and music engraving by Rick Gratton
Cover design by Rick Gratton
Additional editing by Dave Black
Technical assistance: Mike Hoff
Original artwork for the unit titles by Maureen Brown
All photos and videos courtesy of the author

All songs written and performed by Cherry White (www.cherrywhitemusic.com)
Russell Jones - guitars
Ralph Beeby - bass
Felipe Drago - drums

www.wizdom-media.com

WIZDOM MEDIA LLC
48 Troy Hills Rd, Whippany NJ 07981
Copyright ©2016 Wizdom Media LLC
Exclusively distributed by Alfred Music

Inside This Book

Felipe Drago

www.felipedrago.com

Felipe has been playing drums since 1984, turning pro in 1989. He graduated from Musicians Institute (MI), home of the Percussion Institute of Technology (PIT), in Los Angeles, California in the Professional Percussion Player Program in March 1996. Since 1986 he has participated actively in musical groups, working on the stage, in the studio and teaching. His travels include tours of Brazil, Argentina, the South of the USA, and Europe.

Felipe started teaching in 1992, and in 1995 relocated to the USA to study at MI. After graduating, he worked with various artists, in recording sessions and as a teacher at the Eubanks Conservatory of Music and Arts, where in September of 1996 he became the Percussion Department Director. Returning to Brazil in 1998, Felipe started to develop his own teaching method, using his experience as a student at MI and private lessons, and as a teacher. He has written material for absolute beginners covering rock drumming, rudiments, playing techniques and rhythmic reading. All the material uses Accelerative Learning Techniques. These methods were used in the schools where he taught in Brazil.

From 2004 until 2012 Felipe was a very active collaborator of the magazine *Modern Drummer Brasil*. In 2006 Felipe decided to relocate to London in search of new horizons, new challenges and new musical opportunities. Since then Felipe has been teaching, doing session work and live performances. From 2007 until 2012, he was part of the teaching team at The Planet Drum, following which he opened his own teaching practice.

Since 2011 Felipe has been an active member of the rock outfit Cherry White (www.cherrywhitemusic.com) who are being considered the new bearers of the classic rock banner, having recorded two EPs and one full album which have been very well received by the press. In October 2013 Felipe began studying with drummer extraordinaire, drum ambassador and educator Dom Famularo. In March 2014 Felipe went to Paris for the Vic Firth's Private Drum Teachers Seminar, led by Mr. Famularo (and with the presence of the legendary Vic Firth himself). In June of that same year Felipe spent a whole week at the WizDom Drumshed in Long Island, NY with Dom for a period of one-to-one coaching. In 2015, Felipe became a member of the SABIAN Education Network.

Dom Famularo has become more than just a teacher to Felipe; he has become a coach and mentor. Dom has recognized in Felipe competence, capacity and passion in his work, making him part of his selected team of educators and referring him to the education teams of Vic Firth Sticks and Evans Drumheads, two major drum manufacturing companies who are serious about drumming education.

Felipe is a certified representative of Dom's Wizdom Drumshed in London, opening its first franchise in the UK.

ABOUT THE DISC

The included disc is a data disc containing MP3 (audio) and MP4 (video) files. The MP3s are in the root directory of the disc, and the disc should play like a normal CD in most current CD and DVD players. If the MP3s do not play in your CD player, simply place the disc in your computer and import the tracks into iTunes or your favorite music software. You can also play them with Windows Media Player.

The videos are contained in a directory entitled "Play the Drums videos." You will need to place the disc in your computer to access the video files, which are in MP4 format. They will play with QuickTime, Windows Media Player, and many other video player software programs.

All the audio and video files contain the unit and example number to which they refer in the file name.

The following icons are used in the book next to examples that have a play-along track (audio) or video demonstration:

 This icon means there is an accompanying play-along audio MP3 that goes with this example.

 This icon means there is a video demonstration MP4 file on the disc.

AUDIO TRACK LISTING (MP3s)
These files are located in the top directory of the included data disc. They will play like a normal CD in newer CD/MP3 players.

Please note: The examples referred to in the MP3 titles are in the "Play" section of each unit.

1. Half the Time (Unit 1, Example 4, 80 BPM)
2. Half the Time (Unit 1, Example 4, 80 BPM, no drums)
3. The Other Half (Unit 1, Example 6, 80 BPM)
4. The Other Half (Unit 1, Example 6, 80 BPM, no drums)
5. Half and Half (Unit 1, Example 10, 80 BPM)
6. Half and Half (Unit 1, Example 10, 80 BPM, no drums)
7. Sully Street (Unit 2, Example 4, 60 BPM)
8. Sully Street (Unit 2, Example 4, 60 BPM, no drums)
9. Superman (Unit 2, Example 6, 60 BPM)
10. Superman (Unit 2, Example 6, 60 BPM, no drums)
11. Don't Hold Me Back (Unit 2, Example 7, 60 BPM)
12. Don't Hold Me Back (Unit 2, Example 7, 60 BPM, no drums)
13. Empty City (Unit 2, Example 11, 60 BPM)
14. Empty City (Unit 2, Example 11, 60 BPM, no drums)
15. You Need to Move (Unit 2, Example 12, 60 BPM)
16. You Need to Move (Unit 2, Example 12, 60 BPM, no drums)
17. Job in Mind (Unit 3, Example 1, 40 BPM)
18. Job in Mind (Unit 3, Example 1, 40 BPM, no drums)
19. Riding Bikes (Unit 3, Example 10, 40 BPM)
20. Riding Bikes (Unit 3, Example 10, 40 BPM, no drums)
21. Do It Better (Unit 3, Example 14, 40 BPM)
22. Do It Better (Unit 3, Example 14, 40 BPM, no drums)
23. Serenade (Unit 4, Example 3, 50 BPM)
24. Serenade (Unit 4, Example 3, 50 BPM, no drums)
25. Take it Slow (Unit 4, Example 10, 50 BPM)
26. Take it Slow (Unit 4, Example 10, 50 BPM, no drums)
27. Free to Bounce (Unit 4, Example 11, 50 BPM)
28. Free to Bounce (Unit 4, Example 11, 50 BPM, no drums)
29. Elsa Winthrop (Unit 4, Example 19, 50 BPM)
30. Elsa Winthrop (Unit 4, Example 19, 50 BPM, no drums)

VIDEO LISTING (MP4s)

These files are located in the "Play the Drums videos" folder of the included data disc.

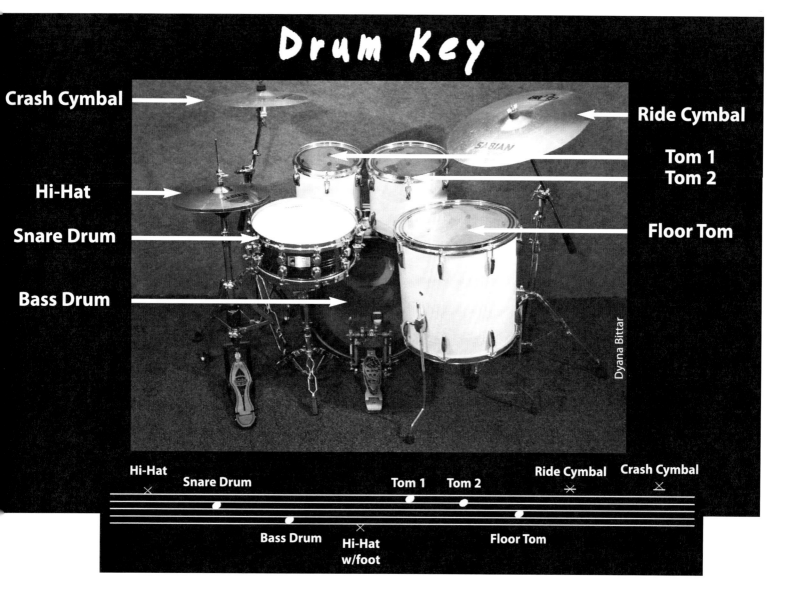

Foreword

Dom Famularo

Dedication is a word that must be seen and shown! Felipe Drago clearly set the path of his constant desire to learn and grow. He wanted to always *Play the Drums*—and be the best he could!

A native of Brazil, performing and teaching there for many years, Felipe moved to London, England, to further his goals. He contacted me to push himself to understand more about his playing and education goals. He flew to Long Island, New York for seven days of lessons at my studio, studying for eight hours a day. He has continued to study as we use Skype to bridge the gap from London to New York! His teaching commitment with a full student schedule keeps him active in sharing what he continues to learn! This is the cycle to not only empower your students, but to constantly keep your skills at the highest level!

Felipe continues to perform with his band and takes on new students. This is dedication! He shows it in every day he embraces music! He put this book together to inspire his students to acquire the skills to *Play the Drums* as fast as they can, to experience the joy he finds in drumming!

You will learn from the videos and audio included with this book. Feel the joy in playing drums and seek your own level of dedication to show others how you *Play the Drums*!

Dom Famularo
Drumming's Global Ambassador
www.domfamularo.com

Joe Bergamini

We are pleased to introduce Felipe Drago's *Play the Drums* as the latest addition to Wizdom's growing catalog. This book will help you get started playing the drums right away!

Felipe is an experienced teacher and his expertise comes through with this book. The book presents the basics of drumming in an organized and simple way. There are four units, with each one divided into Play, Coordination, Reading, Theory, and Fun. These sections cover the specific concepts needed to get a basic understanding of playing the drums.

- Play: These are the basic beats in each unit.
- Coordination: These beats will help you to learn to coordinate your limbs to play the drumset.
- Reading: These exercises will help you learn to read basic drum music.
- Theory: This section explains the various note and rest values and other concepts in the book.
- Fun: Here we put it all together and play some fun beats!

Later units in the book add a section called Extra Practice, which contains some additional, slightly more advanced concepts. One of the coolest things about this book is that Felipe has included 30 play-along tracks for you to have fun playing these beats and fills to music, and 62 videos demonstrating examples from the book. These will really help you learn to play the drums quickly.

Don't forget: Finding a good drum teacher will help you move ahead even faster.

Have fun learning with this great book.

Joe Bergamini
www.joebergamini.com

Play the Drums

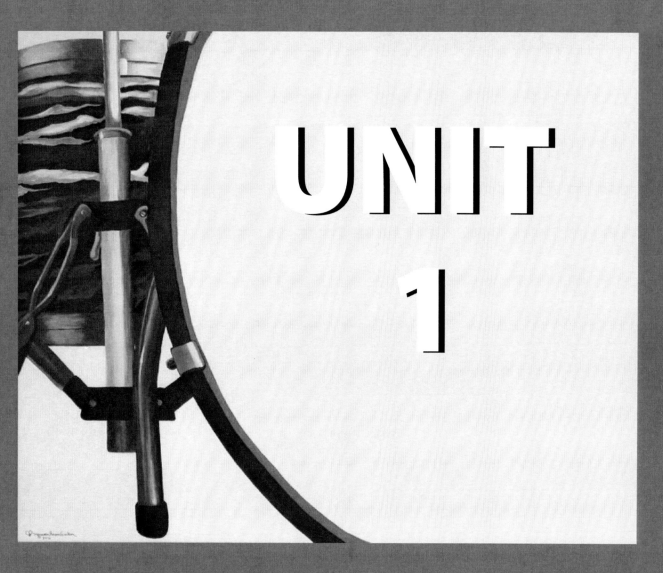

UNIT
1

Count
1 2 3 4

Your fun is about to start.

Don't try to rush, be patient & enjoy the moment.

Use a metronome, start slow and work on your speed gradually.

Count out loud.

Take your time and have fun!

Drum Key

1.

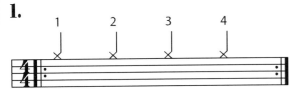

2.

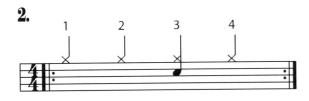

3.

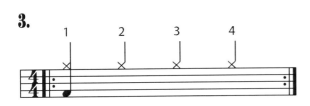

4.

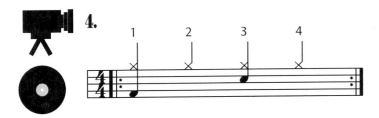

5.

6.

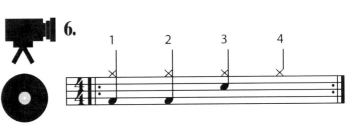

7.

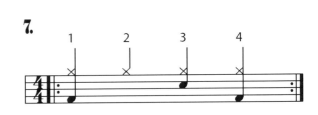

8.

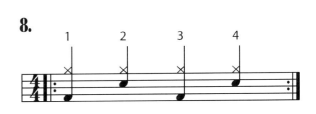

9.

10.

11.

12.
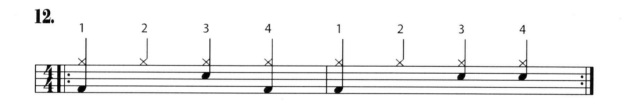

13.

14.

15.
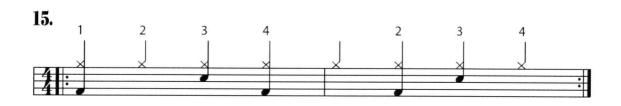

Don't try to rush, be patient & enjoy the moment.

Use a metronome, start slow and work on your speed gradually.

Count out loud.

Take your time and have fun!

Drum Key

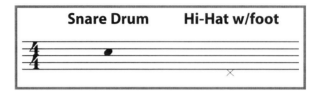

R= Right Hand
L= Left Hand

Single Stroke

1.

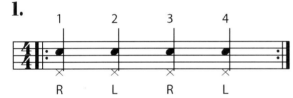

2.

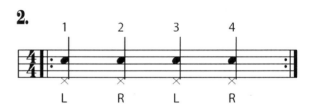

Double Stroke

3.

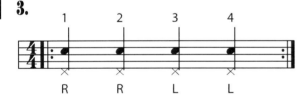

4.

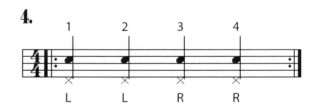

Paradiddle

5.

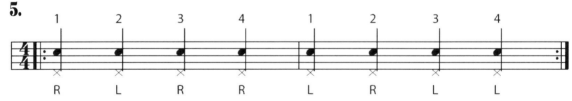

6.

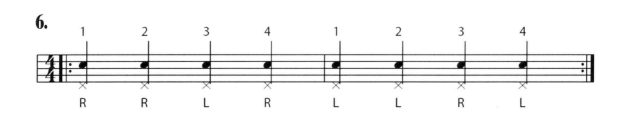

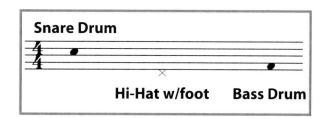

Snare Drum

Hi-Hat w/foot   Bass Drum

7.

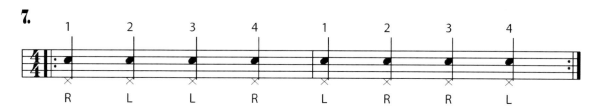

8.

9.

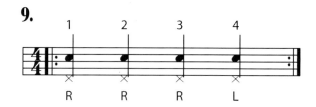

10.

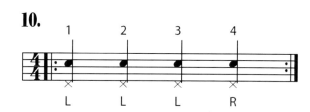

11.

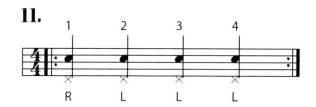

12.

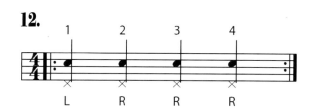

13.

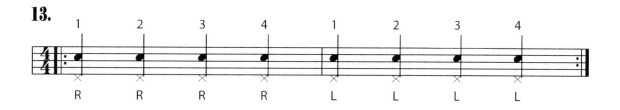

14.

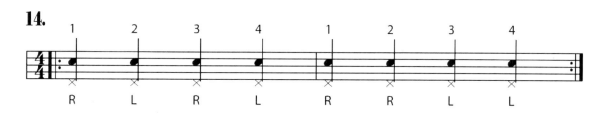

15.

Don't try to rush, be patient & enjoy the moment.

Use a metronome, start slow and work on your speed gradually.

Count out loud.

Take your time and have fun!

Drum Key

| Snare Drum | Quarter Note Rest | Half Note Rest | Whole Note Rest |

1.

2.

3.

4.

5.

6.

7.

Dyana Bittar

Recording with Cherry White

4.1) Notes and Rests

The symbols used to represent rhythm and the duration of the sound are called **notes** and the symbols used to represent the duration of silence are called **rests**. In order to better understand how this works, let's compare one measure to a pizza.

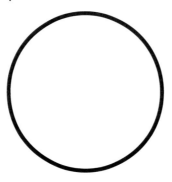

If you don't cut out any slices, you have the entire pizza, and there is a note that fills the entire bar. It is called a **whole note** (in British English it is the semibreve). It looks like this in the bar:

1	2	3	4
o			

In drumming, this means that you play the note and wait a whole bar to play again, as we cannot increase the duration of the notes—but on a saxophone, for example, it means the player has to be blowing the note during all four beats without interruption. Even though as drummers we are not able to make the notes longer with our instrument, we need to learn the same note values as the other musicians. If we see music with whole notes, we can use parts of the drumset that have longer sounds in order to support that note value, or play a roll.

Moving on with our musical pizza, if we cut it in half, we will have, obviously, two halves.

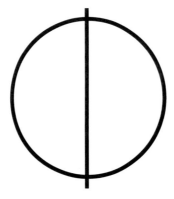

There is also a note that fills half of the bar and it is called a **half note**. (In British English it is the minim.) On the staff it looks like this:

Again, as drummers we wait two beats to play again, while a saxophone player would hold the note for two beats.

Cutting our pizza into four slices gives us four quarters.

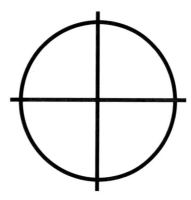

The note that fills only one beat in the bar is called a **quarter note**. (In British English it is the crotchet). It looks like this on the staff:

There are also the symbols that represent the silence with the same duration as the notes, the rests. The **whole-note rest** looks like this:

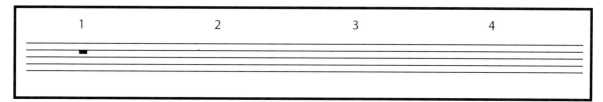

This is the **half-note rest**:

And this is the **quarter-note rest**:

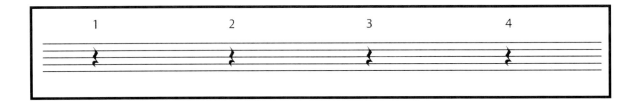

Below is a diagram to give you a clearer view of the relationship between the notes.

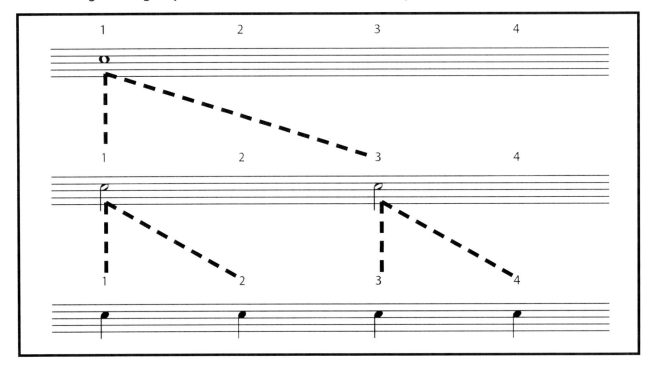

Of course, the same kind of relationship exists between the rests, and as you have seen in reading exercises, the combination of different notes and rests create rhythmic phrases.

Here is the relationship of the rests:

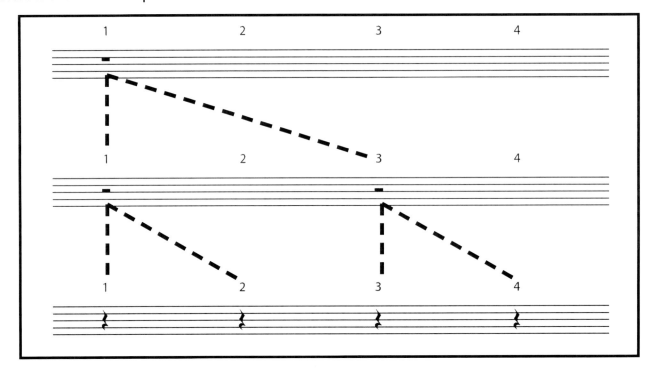

4.2) Staff

The staff is the arrangement of five equidistant horizontal lines where the musical notes are written. The lines and the spaces are counted from the bottom up.

4.3) Barlines

Barlines are vertical lines through the staff used to separate the measures.

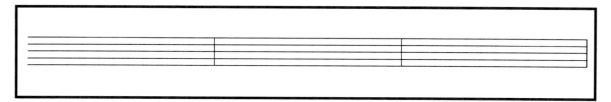

4.4) Measure

The measure is the space between two strong beats separated by a barline. Measures are also referred to as "bars."

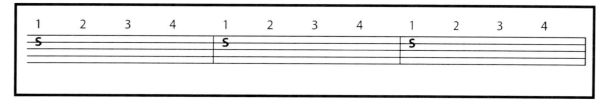

Two barlines close together, referred to as a double barline, are used to indicate the end of a musical section.

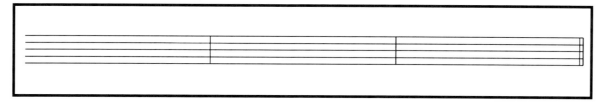

Double barlines with two dots next to them are called repeat signs. The section between these signs is to be repeated.

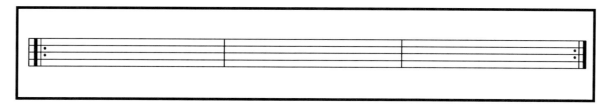

A double barline with one thin and one thick line is used to indicate the end of a composition.

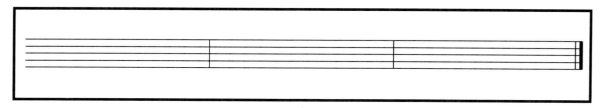

Don't try to rush, be patient & enjoy the moment.

Use a metronome, start slow and work on your speed gradually.

Count out loud.

Take your time and have fun!

Drum Key

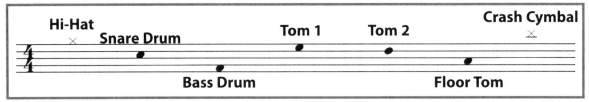

1.

2.

3.

4.

5.

6.

7.

Unit 1 - Songs

This is your first opportunity to play a song on the drums. Savor it! Relax and enjoy the moment. If you have practiced enough you shouldn't have any problems playing these songs. Besides the suggested beats, try others from this unit. See for yourself which ones you think sound and feel the best.

When you're confident enough try incorporating the drum fills from the Fun section.

All the songs in this book are recorded with and without drums for you to practice along. Listen to the version with drums, then try playing along to it. When you are comfortable, move to the version without drums.

Songs:

1. "Half the Time" (suggested beat, exercise 4, pg. 8)

2. "The Other Half" (suggested beat, exercise 6, pg. 8)

3. "Half and Half" (suggested beat, exercise 10, pg. 9)

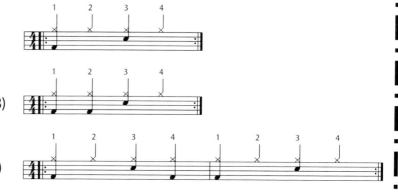

Play the Drums

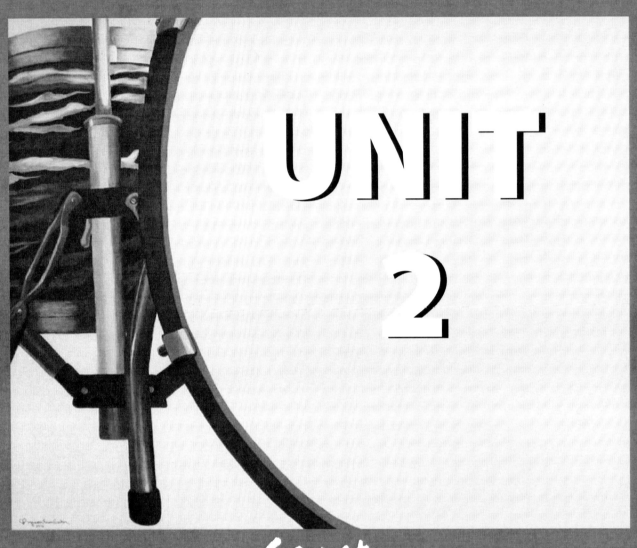

UNIT 2

Count
1 + 2 + 3 + 4 +
("+" pronounced "and")

Your fun is about to start.

Don't try to rush, be patient & enjoy the moment.

Use a metronome, start slow and work on your speed gradually.

Count out loud.

Take your time and have fun!

Drum Key

1.

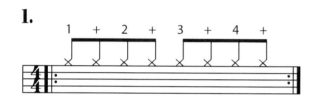

6.

2.

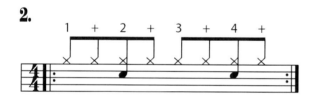

7.

3.

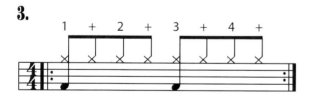

8.

4.

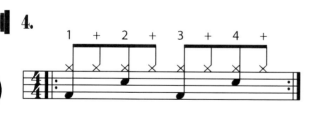

9.

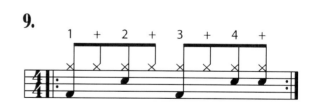

5.

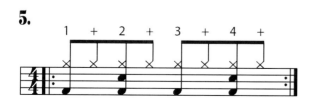

10.

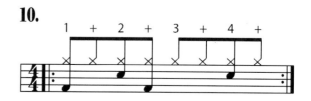

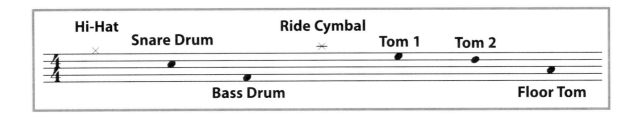

11.

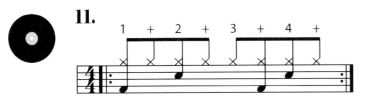

16.

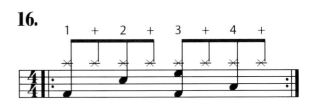

12.

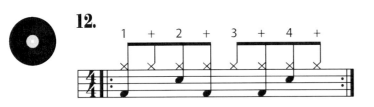

17.

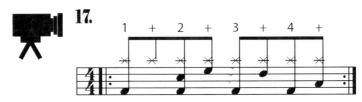

13.

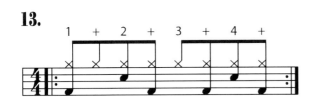

18.

14.

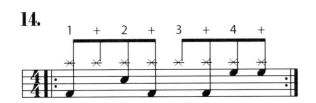

19.

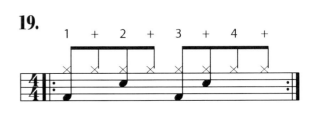

15.

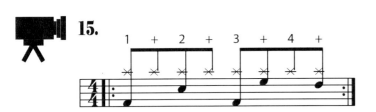

20.

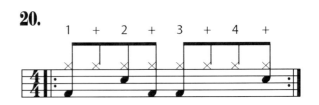

Coordination

Don't try to rush, be patient & enjoy the moment.

Use a metronome, start slow and work on your speed gradually.

Count out loud.

Take your time and have fun!

Drum Key

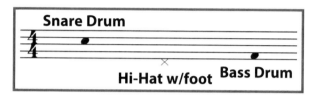

1. Single Stroke

R L R L R L R L

2.

L R L R L R L R

3. Double Stroke

R R L L R R L L

4.

L L R R L L R R

5. Paradiddle

R L R R L R L L

6.

R R L R L L R L

7.

R L L R L R R L

8.

R L R L L R L R

9.

R R R L R R R L

10.

L L L R L L L R

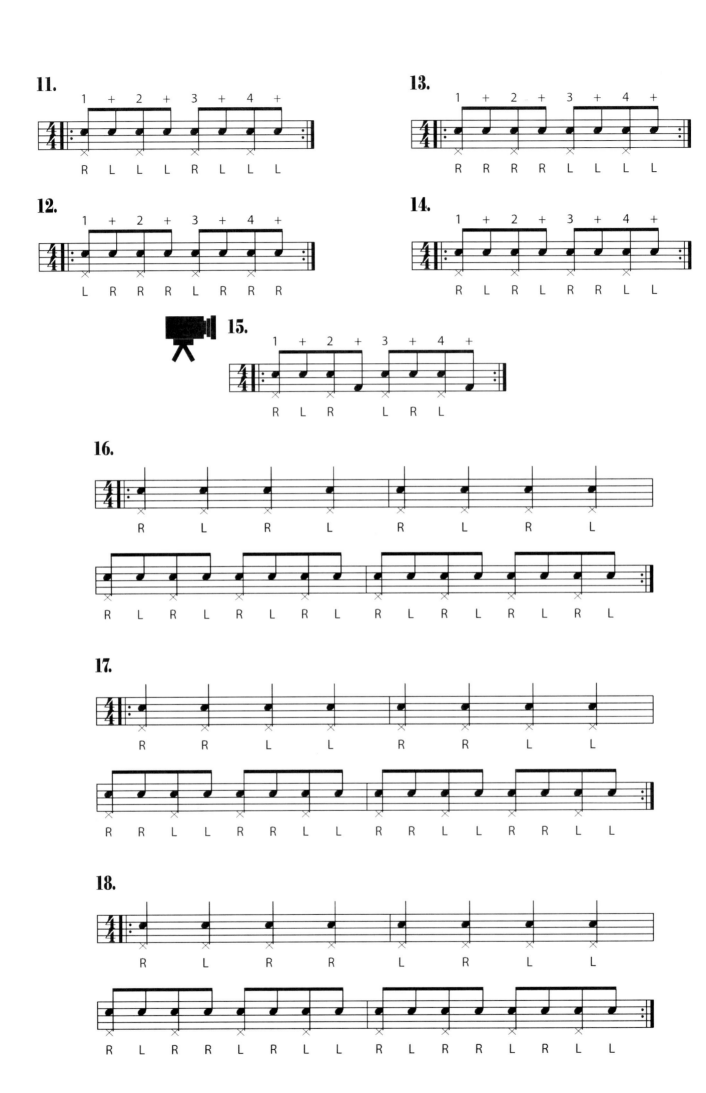

Play the Drums - Unit 2

Don't try to rush, be patient & enjoy the moment.

Use a metronome, start slow and work on your speed gradually.

Count out loud.

Take your time and have fun!

Drum Key

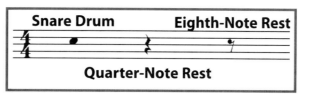

Snare Drum   **Eighth-Note Rest**

Quarter-Note Rest

1.

2.

3.

4.

5.

6.

7.

Dyana Bittar

Play the Drums - Unit 2

4.1) Notes and Rests

Going back to our musical pizza, first we had the whole pizza, then we cut two slices and finished Unit 1 by cutting the pizza into four pieces. Now we are going to cut it into eight slices.

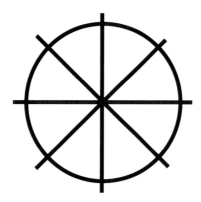

The same way in which we have eight slices of the pizza we can have eight "slices" of the bar, and the note that represents one eighth of the bar is an **eighth note**. (In British English it is the quaver.) It looks like this on the staff:

For each beat of the bar there are two notes. As you can see, you can write them in two different forms: If they are not connected to each other, we write them as they appear in beat 1 of the bar above, but you can also connect them in groups of two and groups of four.

Below you have the **eighth-note rest**. The rests cannot be connected.

And here is a diagram that gives a better view of the relationship between the notes:

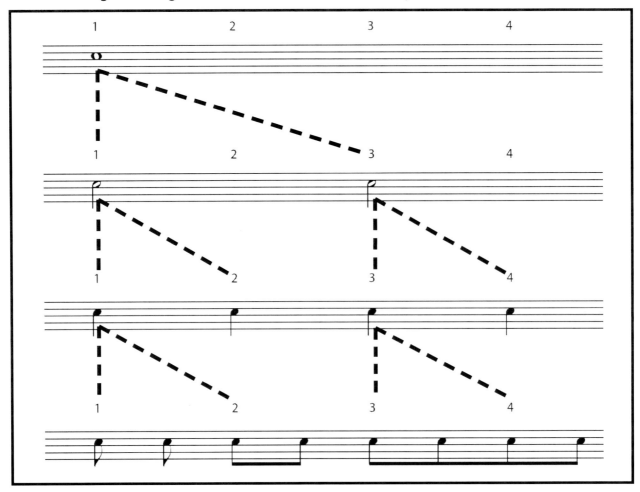

4.2) Counting

Counting is the technique of verbalizing the beats and their subdivisions.

1-Part Counting

This occurs when we only count the beats of the bar, as shown in the example below. This is how we counted in Unit 1.

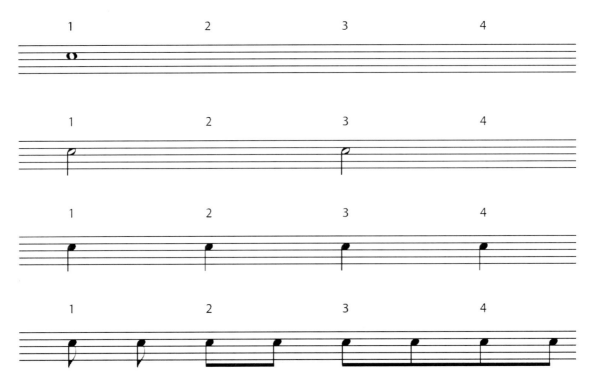

2-Part Counting

This occurs when we subdivide the beat in two, adding the syllable "and" between each number. It is abbreviated in this book with a plus sign (+). This is how the exercises in Unit 2 are counted.

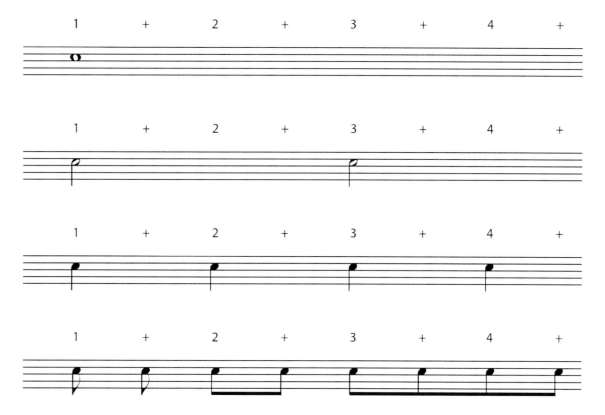

Both techniques can be used in all the exercises in Units 1 & 2. As extra practice, do the reading exercises in Unit 1 using 2-part counting, and the reading exercises in Unit 2 using 1-part counting.

Have fun!

Your fun is about to start.

Don't try to rush, be patient & enjoy the moment.

Use a metronome, start slow and work on your speed gradually.

Count out loud.

Take your time and have fun!

Drum Key

| Hi-Hat | Snare Drum | | Tom 1 | Tom 2 | | Crash Cymbal |

Bass Drum   Floor Tom

1.

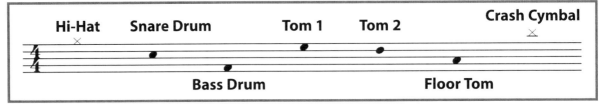

R L

2.

R L R L

3.

Both Hands

4.

R R L L

5.

R L R L

More coordination exercises using quarter and eighth notes.

1.

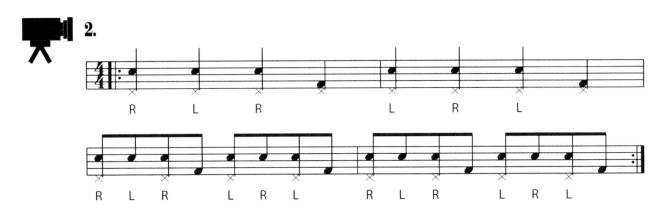

Lesson with Dom at the WizDom Drumshed in Long Island

Now let's play the beats on pages 21 and 22 on the ride cymbal, and keep time with the hi-hat.

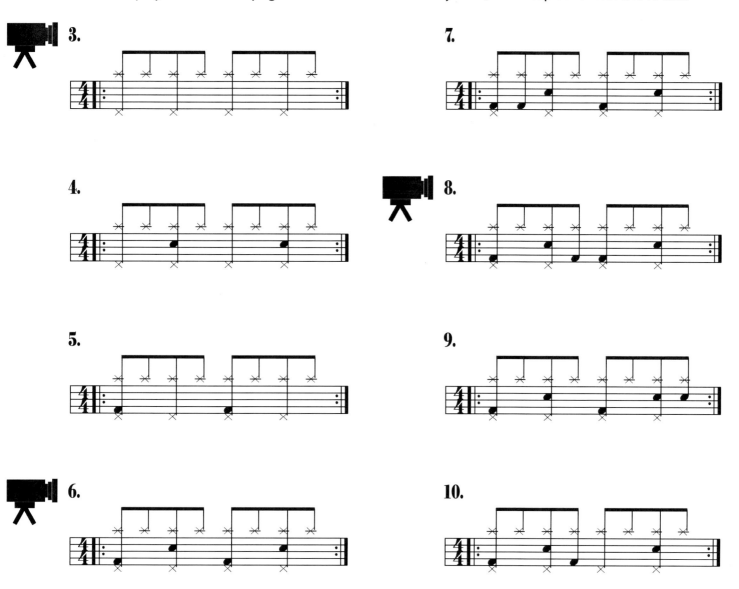

These are some of the beats. Do the same with all of them.

Unit 2 - Songs

Now you're a little more experienced, and playing these songs will come a lot more naturally. I'll risk saying that this is the most important unit—because most of the songs ever recorded have beats with eighth notes on the hi-hat! So take your time getting really comfortable with the beats and the songs. Once you're comfortable playing the songs at the speed they've been recorded, use your favorite app to speed them up and play them faster—but only do that after you can play them well at the recorded speed.

Don't forget to refer to the Fun section of the unit to try some fills on the songs.

Songs:

1. "Sully Street" (suggested beat, exercise 4, pg. 21)

2. "Superman" (suggested beat, exercise 6, pg. 21)

3. "Don't Hold Me Back" (suggested beat, exercise 7, pg. 21)

4. "Empty City" (suggested beat, exercise 11, pg. 22)

5. "You Need to Move" (suggested beat, exercise 12, pg. 22)

Play the Drums

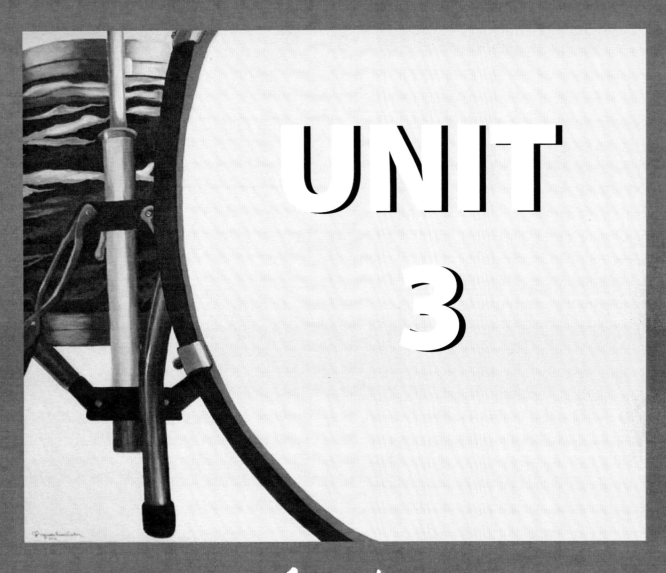

UNIT 3

Count

1 e + a 2 e + a 3 e + a 4 e + a

("a" pronounced "duh")

Your fun is about to start.

Don't try to rush, be patient & enjoy the moment.

Use a metronome, start slow and work on your speed gradually.

Count out loud.

Take your time and have fun!

Drum Key

1.

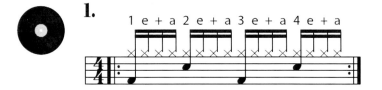

2.

3.

4.

5.

6.

7.

8.

9.

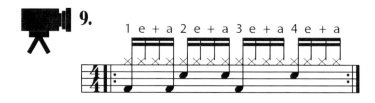

10.

11.

16.

12.
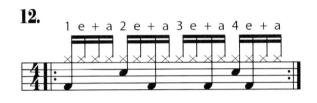

17.
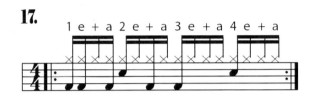

13.

18.

14.

19.

15.

20.

Don't try to rush, be patient & enjoy the moment.

Use a metronome, start slow and work on your speed gradually.

Count out loud.

Take your time and have fun!

Drum Key

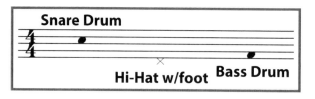

Snare Drum

Hi-Hat w/foot   Bass Drum

1. Single Stroke

1 e + a 2 e + a 3 e + a 4 e + a

R L R L R L R L R L R L R L R L

2.

1 e + a 2 e + a 3 e + a 4 e + a

L R L R L R L R L R L R L R L R

3. Double Stroke

1 e + a 2 e + a 3 e + a 4 e + a

R R L L R R L L R R L L R R L L

4.

1 e + a 2 e + a 3 e + a 4 e + a

L L R R L L R R L L R R L L R R

5. Paradiddle

1 e + a 2 e + a 3 e + a 4 e + a

R L R R L R L L R L R R L R L R

6.

1 e + a 2 e + a 3 e + a 4 e + a

R R L R L L R L R R L R L L R L

7.

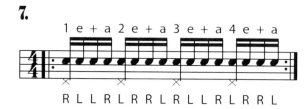

1 e + a 2 e + a 3 e + a 4 e + a

R L L R L R R L R L L R L R R L

8.

1 e + a 2 e + a 3 e + a 4 e + a

R L R L L R L R R L R L L R L R

9.

1 e + a 2 e + a 3 e + a 4 e + a

R R R L R R R L R R R L R R R L

10.

1 e + a 2 e + a 3 e + a 4 e + a

L L L R L L L R L L L R L L L R

11.

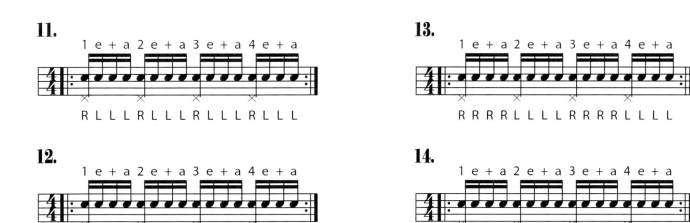

13.

12.

14.

15.

16.

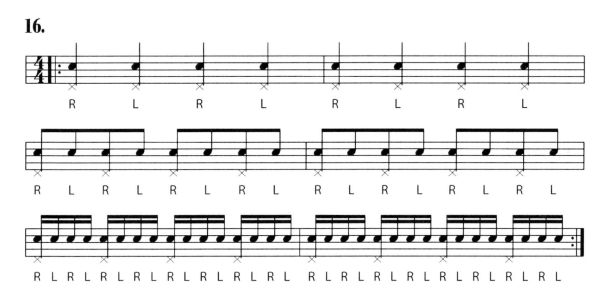

17.

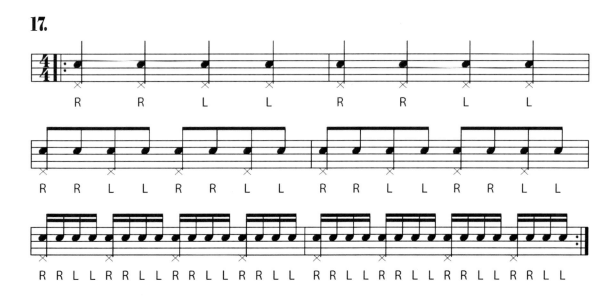

Don't try to rush, be patient & enjoy the moment.

Use a metronome, start slow and work on your speed gradually.

Count out loud.

Take your time and have fun!

Drum Key

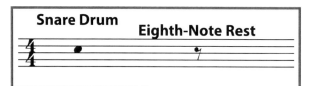

Snare Drum

Eighth-Note Rest

1.

1 e + a 2 e + a 3 e + a 4 e + a   1 e + a 2 e + a 3 e + a 4 e + a

2.

1 e + a 2 e + a 3 e + a 4 e + a   1 e + a 2 e + a 3 e + a 4 e + a

3.

1 e + a 2 e + a 3 e + a 4 e + a   1 e + a 2 e + a 3 e + a 4 e + a

4.

1 e + a 2 e + a 3 e + a 4 e + a   1 e + a 2 e + a 3 e + a 4 e + a

5.

6.

7.

Jessie Leong

Playing live with Cherry White

4.1) Notes and Rests

Once more referring to our musical pizza, we had it as a whole, then we cut two slices and finished Unit 1 by cutting the pizza into four pieces. In Unit 2 we cut it into eight slices. Now we are going to cut it into sixteen pieces.

Applying this concept to the bar, we can have sixteen slices, and the note that represents one sixteenth of the bar is the **sixteenth note**. (In British English it is the semi-quaver.) It looks like this on the staff:

For each beat of the bar there are four notes. As you can see, you can write them in two different forms: If they are not connected to each other, we write them as they appear in beat 1 of the bar above, but you can also connect them in groups of four.

Below you have the **sixteenth-note rests**. The rests cannot be connected.

And here a diagram that gives a better view of the relationship between the notes:

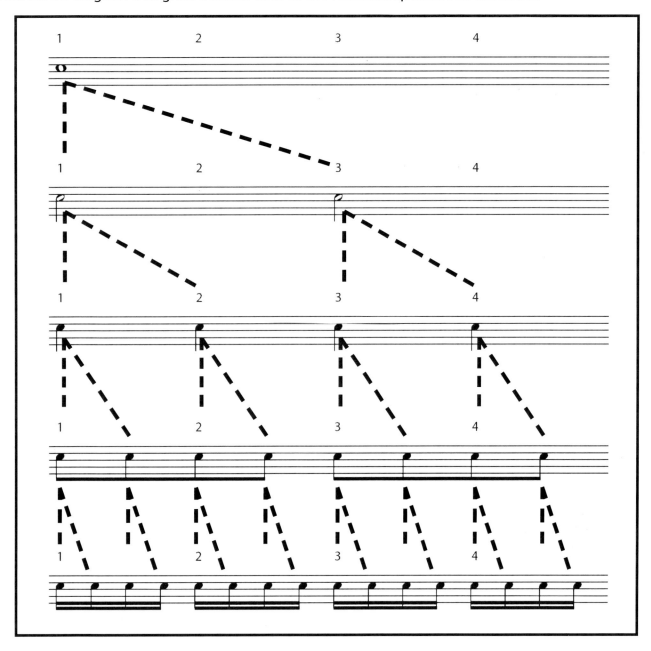

4.2) Counting
4-Part Counting

When we subdivide the beat in four, we add the syllables "e," "and," and "a" (pronounced "ah") between each beat (number).This is how the exercises in Unit 3 are counted.

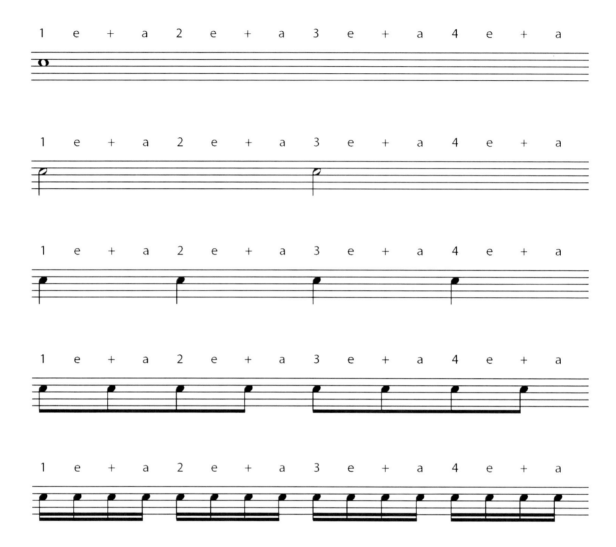

All three counting techniques can be used in all the exercises in the first three units of this book. As extra practice, do the reading exercises in Unit 1 and 2 using 4-part counting, and the reading exercises in Unit 3 using the 1-part and 2-part counting techniques.

Have fun!

Your fun is about to start.

Don't try to rush, be patient & enjoy the moment.

Use a metronome, start slow and work on your speed gradually.

Count out loud.

Take your time and have fun!

Drum Key

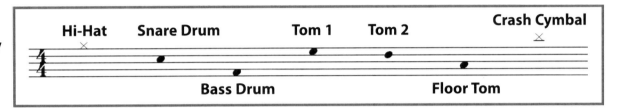

1.

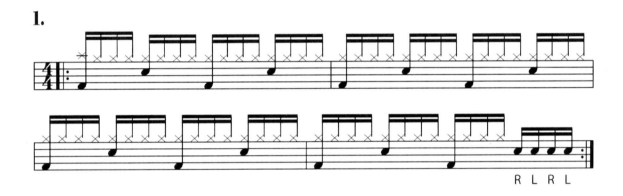

R L R L

2.

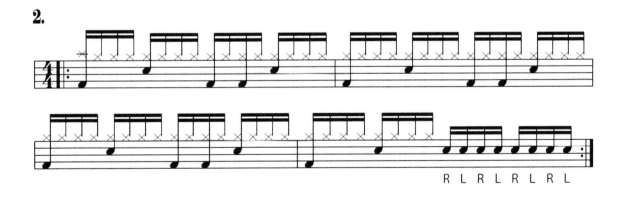

R L R L R L R L

3.

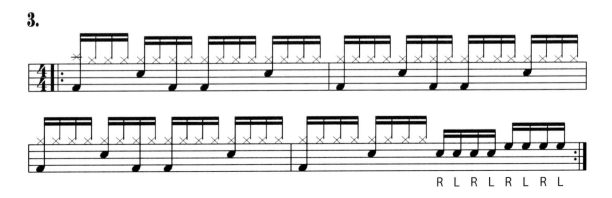

R L R L R L R L

4.

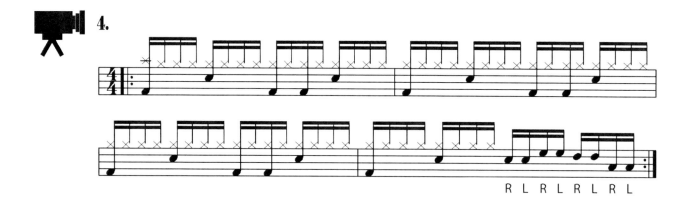

R L R L R L R L

5.

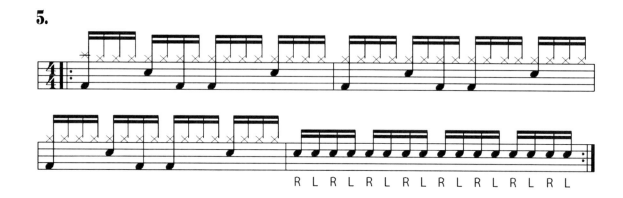

R L R L R L R L R L R L R L R L

6.

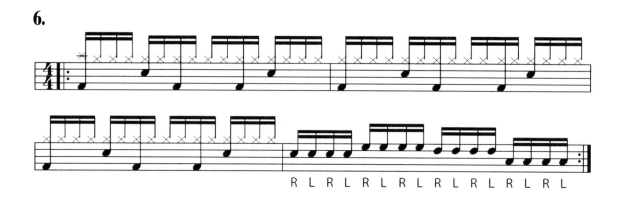

R L R L R L R L R L R L R L R L

7.

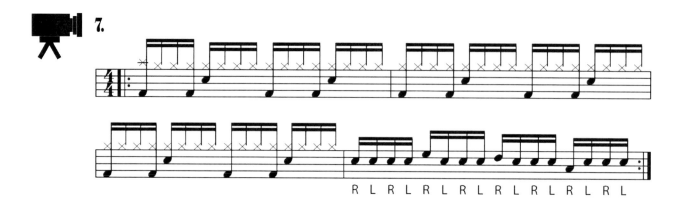

R L R L R L R L R L R L R L R L

8.

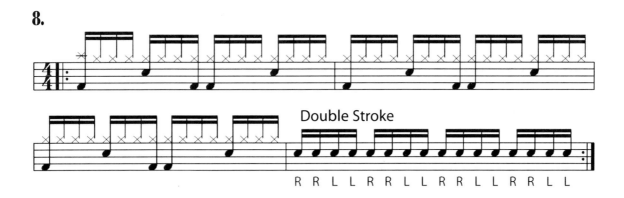

Double Stroke

R R L L R R L L R R L L R R L L

9.

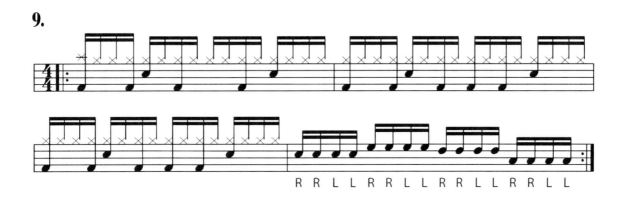

R R L L R R L L R R L L R R L L

10.

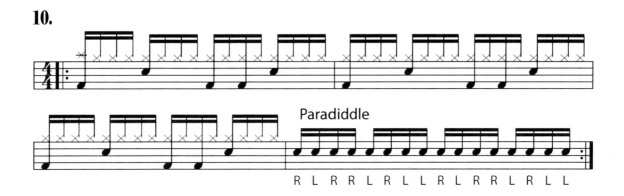

Paradiddle

R L R R L R L L R L R R L R L L

11.

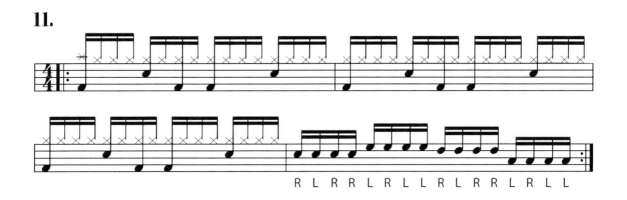

R L R R L R L L R L R R L R L L

1.

2.

3.

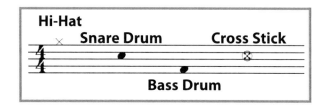

4.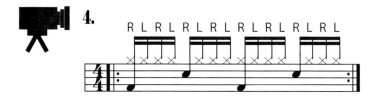

5.

R L R L R L R L R L R L R L R L

6.

R L R L R L R L R L R L R L R L

7.

R L R L R L R L R L R L R L R L

8.

R L R L R L R L R L R L R L R L

9.

10.

R L R L R L R L R L R L R L R L

11.

R L R L R L R L R L R L R L R L

12.

R L R L R L R L R L R L R L R L

Play the rest of the exercises on pages 36 and 37 with the hi-hat played hand-to-hand (R L R L).

13.

Basic Bossa Nova Beat

Unit 3 - Songs

In this unit things get a little more challenging, as sixteenth notes require a lot of precision and stamina to keep a steady beat. These songs are fairly slow to allow you to not only practice the beats but also to make it easier to create a good performance. As you did with the songs in Unit 2, after you're comfortable enough playing them at the original tempo, use an app to speed them up a and make them more exciting.

Refer to the Fun section and apply fills to the songs.

Songs:

1. "Job in Mind" (suggested beat, exercise 1, pg. 36)

2. "Riding Bikes" (suggested beat, exercise 10, pg. 36)

3. "Do it Better" (suggested beat, exercise 14, pg. 37)

With Dom at the MusikMesse in Frankfurt (2014), and Klaus Hessler photobombing at the back

Play the Drums

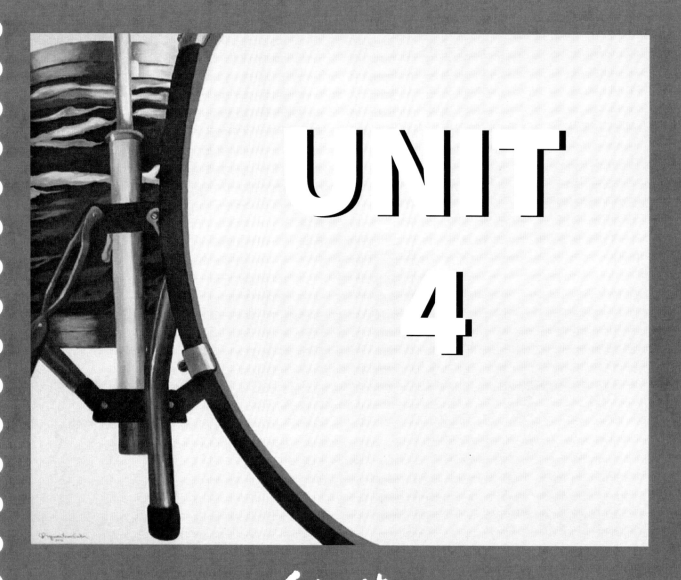

UNIT
4

Count
1 t t 2 t t 3 t t 4 t t
(pronounced "tee" and "ta")

Your fun is about to start.

Don't try to rush, be patient & enjoy the moment.

Use a metronome, start slow and work on your speed gradually.

Count out loud.

Take your time and have fun!

Drum Key

1.

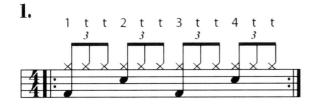

2.

3.

4.

5.

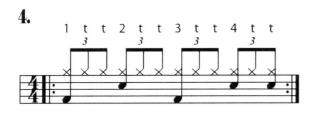

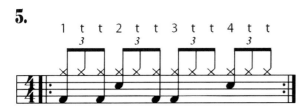

6.

7.

8.

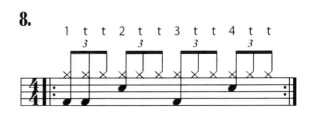

9.

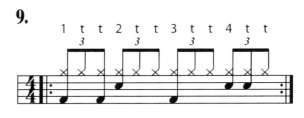

10.

Basic Blues Beat

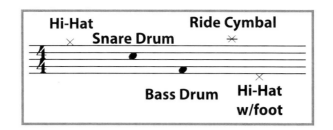

11.

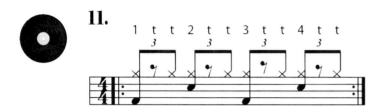

16.

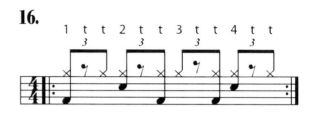

12.

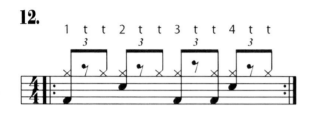

17.

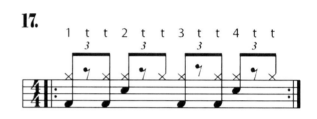

13.

18.

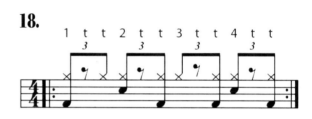

14.

19.

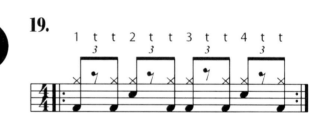

15.

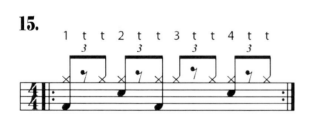

20.

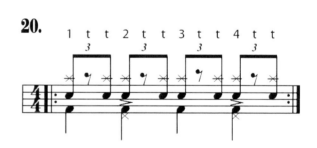

Play the Drums - Unit 4

Coordination

Don't try to rush, be patient & enjoy the moment.

Use a metronome, start slow and work on your speed gradually.

Count out loud.

Take your time and have fun!

Drum Key

Snare Drum

Hi-Hat w/foot   Bass Drum

Single Stroke

1.

Double Stroke

2.

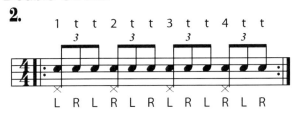

3.

4.

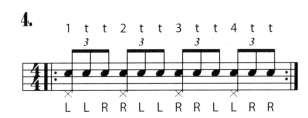

Paradiddle

5.

6.

7.

8.

9.

11.

10.

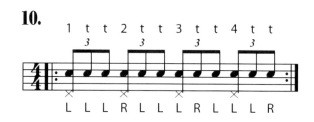

12.

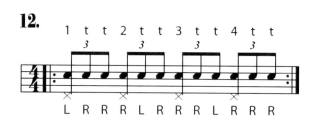

13.

14.

15.

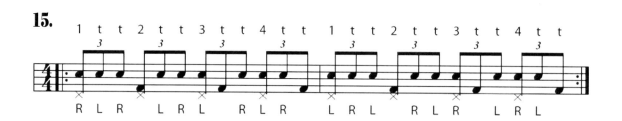

Coordination

Don't try to rush, be patient & enjoy the moment.

Use a metronome, start slow and work on your speed gradually.

Count out loud.

Take your time and have fun!

Drum Key

Snare Drum
Hi-Hat w/foot   Bass Drum

Single Stroke

1.

1 t t 2 t t 3 t t 4 t t

R L R L R L R L R L R L

Double Stroke

2.

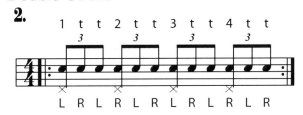

1 t t 2 t t 3 t t 4 t t

L R L R L R L R L R L R

3.

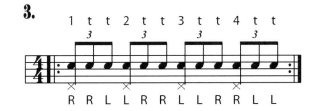

1 t t 2 t t 3 t t 4 t t

R R L L R R L L R R L L

4.

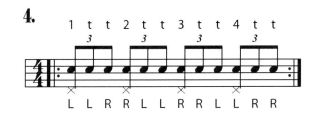

1 t t 2 t t 3 t t 4 t t

L L R R L L R R L L R R

Paradiddle

5.

1 t t 2 t t 3 t t 4 t t   1 t t 2 t t 3 t t 4 t t

R L R R L R L L R L R R   L R L L R L R R L R L L

6.

1 t t 2 t t 3 t t 4 t t   1 t t 2 t t 3 t t 4 t t

R R L R L L R L R R L R   L L R L R R L R L L R L

7.

1 t t 2 t t 3 t t 4 t t   1 t t 2 t t 3 t t 4 t t

R L L R L R L R R L R L   L R R L R L R L L R R L

8.

9.

11.

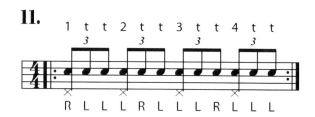

10.

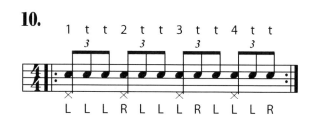

12.

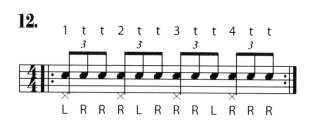

13.

14.

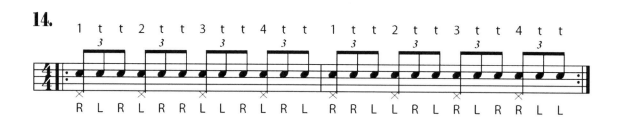

15.

Play the Drums - Unit 4

Reading

Don't try to rush, be patient & enjoy the moment.

Use a metronome, start slow and work on your speed gradually.

Count out loud.

Take your time and have fun!

Drum Key

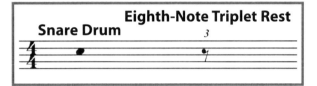

Snare Drum

Eighth-Note Triplet Rest

1.

2.

3.

4.

5.

6

7.

Jessie Leong

Playing live with Cherry White

Play the Drums - Unit 4

4.1) Notes and Rests

So far we have divided our musical pizza in multiples of 2 and 4 (2, 4, 8 and 16 slices). Now we are going to cut it into twelve slices.

Now each beat of our bar has been divided in three, creating what is commonly known as **triplets**. Throughout this unit we have been playing eighth-note triplets. (In British English this is called the quaver triplet.) In order to differentiate the triplets from regular eighth notes, we put the number 3 on top or below the group of notes. Then you will know that instead of two notes per beat you have to play three notes per beat. It looks like this on the staff:

As it happens with the other figures, there is also the rest and it has the same value as the note. It also needs the 3 on top (or below) to indicate the triplet. Note that if the silence is for a whole beat, we use the quarter-note rest (and not three triplet eighth-note rests).

Here is a diagram that gives a better view of the relationship between the quarter note and the eighth-note triplet:

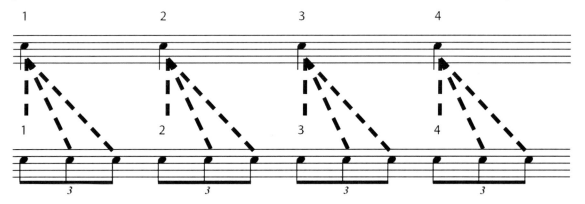

4.2) Counting
3-Part Counting

This occurs when we subdivide the beat into three, adding the syllables "tee" and "ta" between each beat (number). This is how the exercises in Unit 4 are counted.

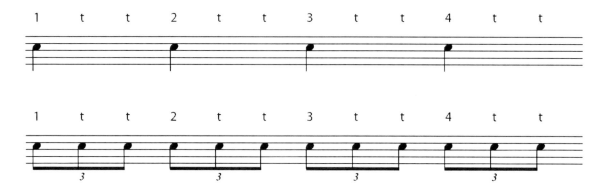

Practice the exercises in this unit using the 3-part and 1-part counting techniques.

Have fun!

With Thabba Coutinho, my 1st drum teacher (2015)

Play the Drums - Unit 4

Fun!

Your fun is about to start.

Don't try to rush, be patient & enjoy the moment.

Use a metronome, start slow and work on your speed gradually.

Count out loud.

Take your time and have fun!

Drum Key

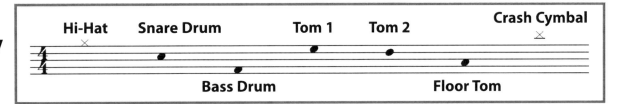

Hi-Hat   Snare Drum   Tom 1   Tom 2   Crash Cymbal

Bass Drum   Floor Tom

1.

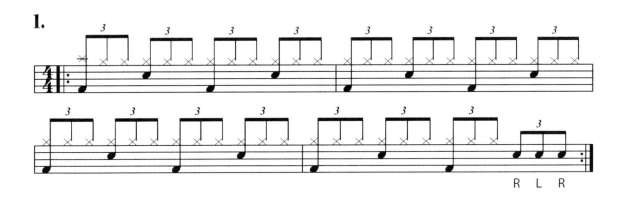

R L R

2.

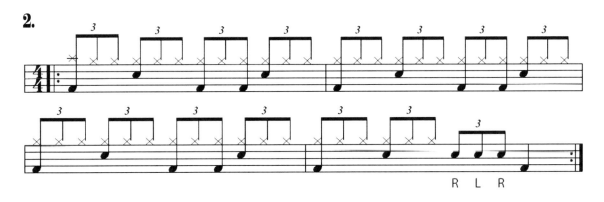

R L R

3.

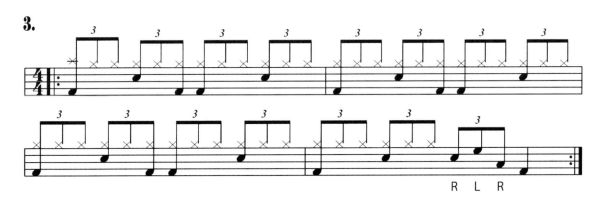

R L R

4.

R L R L R L

5.

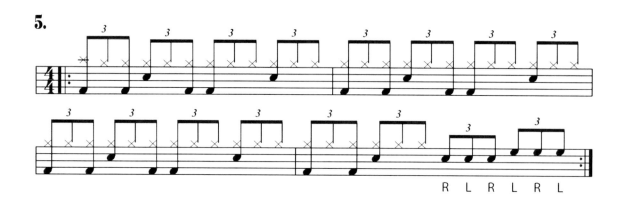

R L R L R L

6.

R L R L R L

7.

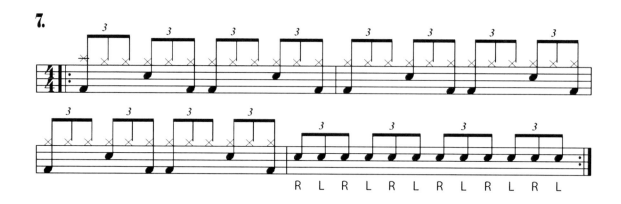

R L R L R L R L R L R L

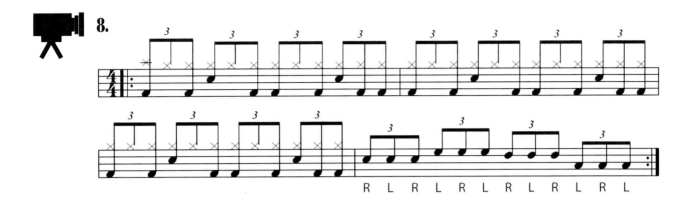

8.

R L R L R L R L R L

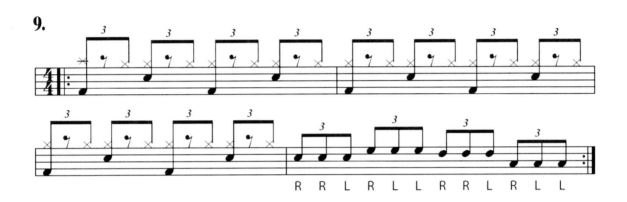

9.

R R L R L L R R L R L L

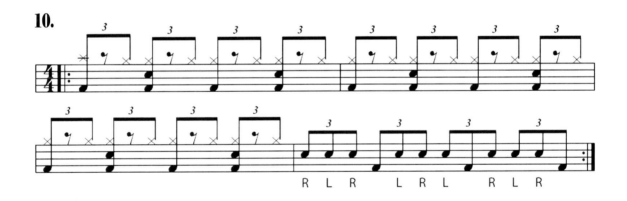

10.

R L R L R L R L R

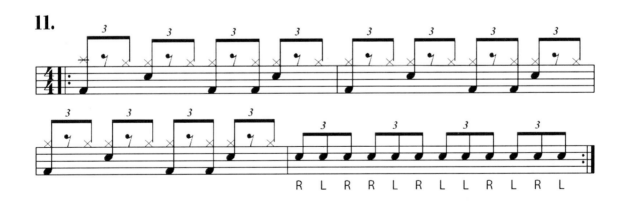

11.

R L R R L R L L R L R L

Extra Practice

1.

2.

3.
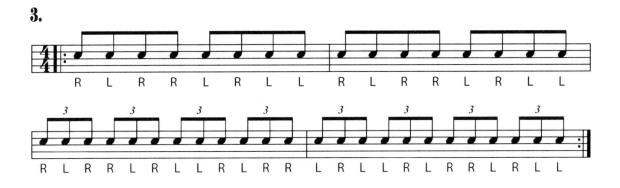

4.

5.

Play the Drums - Unit 4

Unit 4 - Songs

In this unit you're facing some of the most challenging grooves to play, especially the shuffle beats. Make sure that the shuffle beats have a lot of swing and space. Don't worry if you need to practice these songs for a little more time before getting comfortable enough to speed them up. You will only benefit if you take longer to be comfortable with the beats in this unit.

Try as many drum fills as you like from the Fun part of the unit, or create your own.

Songs:

1. "Serenade" (suggested beat, exercise 3, pg. 53)

2. "Take it Slow" (suggested beat, exercise 10, pg. 53)

3. "Free to Bounce" (suggested beat, exercise 11, pg. 54)

4. "Elsa Winthrop" (suggested beat, exercise 19, pg. 54)

With Dom at his WizDom Drumshed in Long Island

The latest great books from Wizdom Media:

NEW! Arrival Drum Play-Along (Book/MP3 Disc) by Joe Bergamini with Dom Famularo: With exciting rock, funk, and progressive tracks taken from Joe's 1996 debut album. Featuring Zak Rizvi and Frank LaPlaca from 4Front, all 10 tracks contain complete charts with suggested grooves and fills, as well as audio versions with drums, minus drums with click, and minus click without drums.

NEW! The Pulse of Jazz (Book/MP3 Disc) by Nic Marcy: A complete, cutting-edge approach to jazz timekeeping from basic to very advanced. Includes extensive audio and video examples, plus play-along tracks!

Odd Feelings (Book/MP3 Disc) by Massimo Russo and Dom Famularo: A complete, easy-to-understand approach to odd time signatures. With play-along tracks, MP3 examples and QuickTime videos.

The Hi-Hat Foot (Book/MP3 Disc) by Garey Williams: Gain faciliy with your weakest limb by practicing this complete set of grooves for rock and funk with practical hi-hat foot patterns.

Drummer's Guide to Big Band (Book/MP3-Video Disc) by Garey Williams: A complete introduction to big band drumming, including chart reading, stylistic tips, catching figures, shuffles, ballads, 3/4, Latin, bass drum technique, and more! Includes 5 complete big band play-along charts.

Open-Handed Playing Vol. 2: A Step Beyond (Book/CD) by Claus Hessler with Dom Famularo: Follow-up to the popular first volume, with clear explanations of the linear and rudimental approaches to OHP. Includes 8 new play-along tracks.

ALSO AVAILABLE:
- *Drumset Duets* by Dom Famularo with Stephane Chamberland (Book/MP3 Disc)
- *Elements* (Book/MP3 Disc) by John Favicchia
- *Pedal Control* (Book/MP3 & Video Disc) by Dom Famularo and Joe Bergamini
- *Open-Handed Playing* (Book/CD) by Claus Hessler with Dom Famularo
- *The Weaker Side* (Book) by Dom Famularo and Stephane Chamberland
- *Eighth-Note Rock and Beyond* (Book/MP3 Disc) by Glenn Ceglia with Dom Famularo
- *Groove Facility* (Book/MP3 & Video Disc) by Rob Hirons and Dom Famularo

WIZDOM MEDIA
www.wizdom-media.com
Wizdom Media LLC
48 Troy Hills Rd, Whippany NJ 07981
Exclusively distributed by Alfred Music Publishing Co.
Available at fine music stores and online retailers